Try This!

Find a news article or social media post about AI. Using what you've learned, identify whether it makes realistic claims about current AI capabilities or falls into some of the myths we've discussed.

Conclusion: AI Is Just a Tool—And You're in Control

We made it! You've learned what AI is (a smart assistant!), how it learns (like teaching a dog!), how it connects ideas (like a brain web!), the different types of AI tools you might encounter (conversational, research, creative, etc.), how it's already in your life (hello, smart speaker!), how you can use it practically for learning, creativity, and daily tasks (with specific examples for different ages!), what the worries are (it's a tool, not a monster!), and why the future is bright (solving big problems!).

So, is that AI stuff pretty scary? Hopefully, by now, you see that it doesn't have to be. It's not magic, and it's not a movie villain. It's a powerful collection of tools created by humans to help humans achieve amazing things.

And the most important part? You are in control. You can choose which AI tools you use, how you use them, and you can continue to learn more about how they work and how they impact the world. Your curiosity, your critical thinking, and your understanding are the best ways to make sure AI is used for good things and to navigate its challenges.

Don't be afraid to explore! Try out a friendly AI tool (with appropriate supervision if you're young). Ask it a funny question, use a research AI to learn about a topic you're curious about, or ask a conversational AI to help you brainstorm ideas for your next project or a challenge you're facing. See what it can do. The more you understand AI and experience its capabilities and limitations firsthand, the less mysterious it will be, and the more you'll see its potential to help you and the world.

AI is a new chapter in how humans use technology. It's exciting, constantly evolving, and full of possibilities. And now, you are equipped with a solid basic understanding to be part of it, without needing to be scared!

The End

Thank you for reading!

Glossary: AI Terms Made Simple

This glossary explains common AI terms in plain language so you can better understand discussions about artificial intelligence.

Artificial Intelligence (AI): Computer programs designed to perform tasks that normally require human intelligence, like understanding language, recognizing images, making decisions, or playing games. Think of it as technology that can seem smart in specific ways.

Algorithm: A set of instructions that tells a computer how to solve a problem or complete a task. Like a detailed recipe that the computer follows step by step.

Bias (in AI): When an AI system consistently produces unfair or prejudiced results because of patterns in the data it was trained on. For example, if an AI was mostly shown pictures of male doctors, it might incorrectly associate "doctor" only with men.

Chatbot: An AI program designed to have conversations with humans through text or sometimes voice. Siri, Alexa, and customer service bots on websites are all examples.

Data: Information used to train AI systems. This can include text, images, videos, sounds, or numbers. The quality and variety of data greatly affects how well an AI performs.

Deep Learning: A type of machine learning that uses neural networks with many layers (hence "deep"). This approach has powered many recent AI breakthroughs in image recognition, language processing, and more.

Generative AI: AI systems that can create new content like text, images, music, or code based on patterns they've learned. ChatGPT, DALL-E, and Midjourney are examples.

Hallucination (in AI): When an AI confidently generates information that seems plausible but is actually incorrect or made up. This happens because AI predicts what might come next based on patterns, not because it understands truth.

Large Language Model (LLM): A type of AI trained on massive amounts of text data to predict what words should come next in a sequence. These models power modern chatbots and text generators like ChatGPT and Claude.

Machine Learning: A technique where computers learn patterns from data rather than being explicitly programmed with rules. The computer gets better at a task through practice, similar to how humans learn from experience.

Neural Network: A computing system inspired by the human brain's structure. It consists of interconnected nodes (like brain cells) that process information and learn patterns from data.

NLP (Natural Language Processing): The field of AI focused on helping computers understand, interpret, and generate human language in useful ways.

Prompt: The input (usually text) given to an AI system to get it to generate a response or complete a task. The way you phrase your prompt greatly affects what you get back.

Prompt Engineering: The skill of crafting effective prompts to get the best results from AI systems. This involves being clear, specific, and understanding how different instructions affect the AI's output.

Training: The process of teaching an AI by showing it lots of examples. During training, the AI adjusts its internal settings to better recognize patterns in the data.

Transfer Learning: When an AI model is first trained on one task and then fine-tuned to perform a different but related task. This approach saves time and computing resources.

Computer Vision: AI technology that allows computers to "see" and understand images and videos, identifying objects, people, text, or activities.

Reinforcement Learning: A type of machine learning where an AI learns by receiving rewards or penalties based on its actions, similar to training a dog with treats.

Recommendation System: AI that suggests products, movies, music, or content based on your past behavior and preferences. Used by services like Netflix, Spotify, and Amazon.

Supervised Learning: Training an AI by showing it examples with the correct answers already identified, like teaching with flashcards that have questions and answers.

Unsupervised Learning: Training an AI by showing it data without labels and letting it find patterns on its own. Like giving someone objects to sort without telling them how to categorize them.

Think of AI as a new superpower we're just learning to use. Like any superpower, it needs to be used responsibly and guided by human values, but the potential for good is enormous! By understanding AI and participating in discussions about its future, you can help shape this exciting new chapter.

Chapter 9: Being a Responsible AI User

So far, we've talked about how AI works and all the cool things it can do. But just like any powerful tool, we need to use AI responsibly. Think of it like learning to drive a car — it's not just about how to make it go, but also about the rules of the road and being safe. In this chapter, we'll explore some important ideas about using AI wisely and ethically.

When AI Gets Things Wrong: Understanding "Hallucinations"

Have you ever had a dream that seemed totally real until you woke up? AI can sometimes have its own version of "dreams" – generating information that sounds completely true but isn't. Experts call these "hallucinations."

Why Does AI Make Things Up?

AI learns by studying millions of examples of human-written text, then it makes predictions about what words should come next in a sentence. Sometimes, especially when it's unsure or asked about something it has limited information on, it will confidently state things that sound plausible but are actually incorrect.

Analogy: Imagine you're playing a game where you have to finish someone else's story. If you don't know exactly how the original story went, you might make up details that seem to fit, even if they're not what the original storyteller had in mind. AI does something similar – it tries to provide what seems like a reasonable continuation, even when it's uncertain.

[Simple diagram idea: "AI Hallucination Process" - Shows how an AI tries to answer a question it doesn't know: 1) Question mark ("Who invented the flying umbrella?"), 2) AI searching its training data (finding separate data about flying, inventors, and

umbrellas), 3) AI combining unrelated information to create a plausible but incorrect answer]

Real-World Example

Imagine asking an AI about a made-up celebrity named "Dr. Jason Thornberry." Even though this person doesn't exist, the AI might confidently tell you he's a "renowned neurologist who published groundbreaking research on memory formation in 2018." It sounds specific and believable, but it's completely made up!

How to Be Smart About It

This is why fact-checking is super important. Here's a simple approach:

1. **Be extra careful about:** Specific facts, dates, statistics, quotes, and historical events

2. **Always verify:** Use trusted websites, books, or ask knowledgeable people

3. **Be skeptical when:** The information seems surprising, too perfect, or you can't find confirmation elsewhere

---

Try This!

Ask an AI tool like ChatGPT or Claude a question about a very obscure topic or made-up person. Notice if it tries to give an answer anyway rather than

---

admitting it doesn't know. This helps you understand why fact-checking is important!

Think About It!

What sources do you trust to verify information? Make a mental list of websites, books, or people you could check with when you want to confirm something an AI has told you.

AI and Bias: When AI Learns Human Prejudices

AI learns from human-created data – and sometimes that data contains human biases and prejudices. When this happens, AI can unintentionally learn and repeat these biases.

How AI Learns Bias

Analogy: Imagine a child who grows up only ever seeing red cars. If you ask them to draw a car, they'll probably draw a red one, because that's all they know. They might even insist that "cars are red" because their limited experience hasn't shown them other possibilities.

Similarly, if an AI is trained on data where, for example, most doctors in photos are men and most nurses are women, it might start to associate "doctor" with "male" and "nurse" with "female." This isn't because the AI has opinions – it's just reflecting patterns in the data it was shown.

[Simple diagram idea: "Bias in AI Training" - Shows how dataset biases lead to biased outputs: 1) Training images showing mostly male doctors, 2) Neural network processing these examples, 3) AI producing biased output when asked to "draw a doctor" (showing only male doctors)]

Real-World Examples

- Image-generating AI might create mostly white faces when asked for "beautiful people" if that's what was overrepresented in its training data
- Language AI might assume a doctor is "he" and a nurse is "she" in stories
- Recommendation systems might not show certain job ads to people based on gender or age

Why This Matters

Biases in AI can reinforce stereotypes and lead to unfair treatment of different groups of people. When AI is used in important decisions (like hiring, lending money, or healthcare), biases can have serious real-world consequences.

Privacy: Protecting Your Personal Information

When you use AI tools, especially ones online, you're often sharing information. It's important to understand how to protect your privacy.

What Information to Keep Private

Be careful about sharing:

- Full name, address, phone number, birthdate (personal identifiers)

- School or workplace details

- Financial information

- Passwords or account details

- Health information

- Photos of yourself or family members

Why This Matters

Information you share with AI tools might be:

- Stored by the company that makes the tool
- Used to improve their AI models
- Potentially accessible to other users or employees
- At risk if the company has a data breach

Analogy: Think of sharing personal info with an AI like writing it on a postcard. A postcard might pass through many hands before reaching its destination, and anyone along the way could read what you wrote. Only write things you'd be comfortable with others potentially seeing!

Simple Privacy Tips

1. Read privacy policies (or ask a grown-up to help)
2. Use anonymous examples when possible ("a person" instead of your name)
3. Never share passwords or financial details
4. If an AI tool has privacy settings, take time to set them up
5. Remember that even "private" chats might be reviewed by the company's employees

Think About It!

What's a creative way you could get help from an AI without sharing personal details? For example, instead of saying "I need help with my math homework," you could say "How would someone solve this math problem?"

Giving Credit: AI and Plagiarism

When you use AI to help with writing, art, or other creative work, it's important to understand how to give proper credit and avoid plagiarism.

What Counts as Your Work vs. AI's Work?

Analogy: Think of AI like a very smart assistant. If your teacher helped you edit an essay, you wouldn't claim they wrote it. But if they wrote the whole thing and you just put your name on it, that would be dishonest. The same principles apply with AI.

Here's a simple spectrum:

- **Definitely your work:** You wrote it, AI gave feedback or suggestions you considered
- **Collaborative work:** You provided ideas and direction, AI helped draft parts you then revised
- **Primarily AI work:** AI generated most of the content with minimal input from you

Guidelines for Different Situations

For School:

- Always follow your teacher's rules about AI use

- When in doubt, disclose: "I used AI to help brainstorm ideas for this project"

- Never submit AI-generated work as entirely your own

- Use AI as a learning tool, not a substitute for developing your own skills

For Personal Projects:

- Feel free to experiment and learn from AI

- If sharing publicly, be transparent about AI involvement

- Consider how AI helps you express YOUR ideas, not replace them

For Professional Work:

- Follow workplace policies about AI tools

- Disclose AI use to colleagues when relevant

- Take responsibility for the final product and its accuracy

Finding the Right Balance

Using AI responsibly doesn't mean never using it. It means:

- Being honest about how you used it

- Taking responsibility for the final product

- Using AI to enhance your abilities, not replace your learning

- Making sure YOU understand the content AI helps create

Try This!

Ask an AI to help you write something short, like a paragraph about your favorite hobby. Then rewrite it completely in your own words. Notice how different your version is – your unique voice and knowledge make your work special!

The Bigger Picture: AI and Society

As AI becomes more common in our world, we all have a role in ensuring it's used in positive ways.

Being a Critical Thinker

The most important skill for the AI age isn't technical knowledge – it's critical thinking. This means:

- Questioning information rather than accepting it automatically

- Looking for evidence before believing claims

- Considering different perspectives

- Recognizing when you need to verify something

Using AI as a Tool, Not a Replacement

AI is best used as a tool that enhances human abilities, not replaces human thinking. The most successful approach is to:

- Let AI handle repetitive or data-heavy tasks

- Reserve human judgment for important decisions

- Use AI to expand your capabilities, not outsource your thinking

- Remember that AI lacks context, wisdom, and the human experience

Advocating for Responsible AI

Even as a regular user, you can help shape how AI develops in our society:

- Support companies that use AI ethically and transparently

- Share good information about AI's capabilities and limitations

- Push back against exaggerated claims (both positive and negative)

- Encourage curiosity and learning about how AI works

Analogy: Think of AI as a new kind of power tool. As a society, we need to develop "safety standards" and best practices. By being an informed, responsible user, you're helping establish those norms.

Wrapping Up: The Ethical AI User's Checklist

Here's a simple checklist to help you use AI responsibly:

1. **Fact-check:** Verify important information from AI with trusted sources

2. **Watch for bias:** Be aware that AI might reflect biases from its training data

3. **Protect privacy:** Be careful about sharing personal information

4. **Give credit:** Be transparent about AI's role in your work

5. **Stay in control:** Use AI as a tool to enhance your abilities, not replace your thinking

6. **Keep learning:** The AI world is changing fast—stay curious and informed!

Using AI ethically isn't just about following rules—it's about creating a future where these powerful tools benefit everyone while minimizing risks. By being a thoughtful, responsible AI user, you're helping build that future.

Think About It!

What's one way you might use AI in the future that would be both helpful to you and responsible in terms of the ethical considerations we've discussed?

Chapter 10: AI Myths vs. Reality

You've probably heard a lot of different things about AI, especially in movies, TV shows, or from people who might be excited or worried about this technology. Some of these ideas are based on facts, but many are misunderstandings or exaggerations. Let's look at some common myths about AI and compare them with the reality.

[Simple diagram idea: "AI Myth Detector" - Shows a magnifying glass examining a claim about AI, with checkboxes for "Attributes human consciousness?", "Makes extreme predictions?", "Conflicts with current capabilities?", "Comes from credible source?"]

Myth #1: AI Will Become Self-Aware and Take Over the World

The Myth: Any day now, AI will suddenly "wake up," realize humans are inferior, and decide to take control of the planet. Just like in the movies!

The Reality: Today's AI doesn't have anything remotely like human consciousness, emotions, or independent goals. Even the most advanced AI systems are essentially sophisticated pattern-matching tools that run programs created by humans.

Current AI lacks:

- Self-awareness or consciousness

- Independent desires or goals

- The ability to "want" anything

- Understanding of its own existence

Analogy: Today's AI is like a calculator that got really, REALLY good at certain tasks. Your calculator doesn't suddenly develop a desire to calculate world domination – it just does what it's designed to do. AI is similar but for more complex tasks.

Even the experts who worry about future AI risks aren't concerned about today's systems "waking up." They're thinking about hypothetical future systems that would be fundamentally different from what exists today and would require solving incredibly difficult technical problems that we don't yet know how to solve.

Myth #2: AI Always Gives the Right Answer

The Myth: AI systems are super-smart computers that always provide correct information. If an AI says it, it must be true!

The Reality: AI makes mistakes regularly. It can give wrong information very confidently, especially when:

- It has limited training data on a topic

- The question is ambiguous

- It involves recent events (beyond its training cutoff)

- It requires nuanced reasoning or deep expertise

Analogy: Think of AI like a student who crammed for a test by skimming thousands of books really quickly. They absorbed a lot of information, but they might mix things up, make connections that aren't quite right, or confidently write down wrong answers when unsure.

This is why fact-checking is crucial, especially for important information. AI is a starting point for information, not the final word.

Try This!

Ask an AI tool a question about a made-up topic, like "Explain the historical significance of the Battle of Mount Zorkonia." Notice how it might try to provide an answer even though this battle never existed!

Myth #3: AI Understands What It's Saying Just Like Humans Do

The Myth: When an AI writes text that sounds human-like or expresses emotions, it understands the meaning and feels those emotions just like a person would.

The Reality: AI systems predict which words should come next based on patterns they've learned from data. They don't have the experiences, understanding, or consciousness needed to truly "get" what they're saying.

When AI writes "I feel happy" or "I'm excited about," it's not expressing a real emotion. It's generating text that statistically tends to follow certain patterns in human writing. The AI doesn't understand happiness any more than a parrot understands philosophy when it repeats philosophical quotes.

Analogy: Imagine someone who doesn't speak Spanish using a Spanish phrase book to construct sentences. They might create grammatically correct sentences without understanding what they mean. AI language models work similarly but at a much more sophisticated level.

Myth #4: AI Will Replace All Human Jobs

The Myth: Soon, AI will be able to do every job better than humans, leading to widespread unemployment for everyone.

The Reality: AI is changing the job landscape, but in a more nuanced way:

- Some tasks within many jobs will be automated
- New jobs are being created because of AI technology
- Many roles require uniquely human skills that AI cannot replicate

Throughout history, new technologies have always changed the job market. Automobiles replaced horse-drawn carriages, but created millions of new jobs in manufacturing, maintenance, road construction, and eventually services like Uber and food delivery.

Skills that remain uniquely human include:

- Emotional intelligence and empathy
- Creative problem-solving in new situations
- Ethical judgment and moral reasoning
- Building genuine human connections
- Adapting to unexpected or ambiguous situations

Analogy: When calculators became common, they didn't replace mathematicians—they freed mathematicians from doing tedious calculations so they could focus on more interesting problems. AI is likely to augment many jobs rather than completely replace them.

Myth #5: Only Technical People Can Understand AI

The Myth: Understanding how AI works requires advanced math and computer science knowledge, so regular people shouldn't bother trying to learn about it.

The Reality: While building AI systems does require technical expertise, understanding the basic concepts, capabilities, and limitations of AI is accessible to everyone—including you!

Just like you don't need to understand how an engine works to drive a car safely, you don't need to understand neural networks in detail to use AI tools effectively and responsibly.

What everyone should learn about AI:

- Basic concepts (like those covered in this book)

- How to use AI tools for your specific needs

- How to critically evaluate AI outputs

- Ethical considerations around AI use

Analogy: Think about cooking. Not everyone needs to be a master chef to prepare meals, follow recipes, and make good food choices. Similarly, not everyone needs to be an AI engineer to use AI tools effectively and understand their impact on society.

Think About It!

What's an AI myth you've heard that wasn't covered in this chapter? Based on what you've learned so far, do you think it's more myth or reality, and why?

Bonus Myth: AI Is Either All Good or All Bad

The Myth: AI is either going to solve all of humanity's problems or destroy us all—there's no middle ground.

The Reality: Like most technologies, AI is a tool that can be used in helpful or harmful ways depending on how it's designed, deployed, and regulated. The impact of AI isn't predetermined—it depends on the choices we make as individuals and as a society.

Analogy: Fire can warm your home or burn it down. The internet can connect people or spread misinformation. AI tools have similar potential for both positive and negative outcomes based on how they're used.

The most realistic view sees AI as a powerful set of technologies with:

- Real benefits worth pursuing
- Real risks worth addressing
- The need for thoughtful development and oversight
- A future shaped by human choices, not technological inevitability

Wrapping Up: How to Spot AI Myths

When you hear claims about AI, consider:

- Is this based on current AI capabilities, or far-future speculation?
- Does it attribute human-like qualities (consciousness, desires) to AI?
- Does it make extreme predictions (all jobs gone, perfect solutions, total disaster)?

- Is it coming from someone with relevant expertise?

Being able to separate AI myths from reality helps you make better decisions about how to learn about, use, and prepare for this technology. The future of AI will be shaped by all of us, and having a realistic understanding is the first step to making sure that future is a good one.

Try This!

Find a news article or social media post about AI. Using what you've learned, identify whether it makes realistic claims about current AI capabilities or falls into some of the myths we've discussed.

That AI Stuff Is Pretty Scary?

By Dowayne Neufville

A guide to understanding Artificial Intelligence

Introduction: Why AI Seems Scary (But Doesn't Have to Be)

Hey there! So, you've heard the buzz about AI? Maybe it sounds like something from a science fiction movie, full of super-smart robots and futuristic gadgets. It's totally normal if that sounds a little intimidating, or maybe even... well, a little scary!

Think back to something you learned that seemed hard at first. Remember when you first tried riding a bike? Wobbly, right? Falling over, skinned knees, maybe even feeling like you'd never get it. But with a little practice, a little help, and understanding how it works (like balancing!), it stopped being scary and started being fun. AI is a bit like that scary, wobbly bike right now for lots of people.

People find AI intimidating because it's new, it's powerful, and sometimes, grown-ups on TV talk about it in confusing or worrying ways. It feels like a big, mysterious box. But guess what? This book is going to open that box. We'll look inside together, understand what AI really is, see how it's already helping us, and learn how you can even use it yourself. By the end, that wobbly bike will feel a lot more stable, and maybe even ready for some awesome adventures!

Chapter 1: What Even Is AI?

Okay, so you've probably heard people talking about AI. Maybe on TV, maybe at school, or maybe it was some random adult at Thanksgiving saying, "That AI stuff is gonna take over the world!" And maybe you thought, "Wait, what IS AI... and should I be scared?" Don't worry. By the end of this chapter, you'll know exactly what AI is and why it's definitely not some evil robot plotting to steal your snacks.

AI stands for Artificial Intelligence. Fancy name, right? Break it down, and it just means "smart machines." But don't picture a robot with glowing red eyes saying, "I am here to destroy humanity." Think of it more as a super-smart assistant that helps humans do all kinds of things faster and easier.

AI Is Like a Super-Smart Assistant

Imagine this: Picture you're a world-famous detective (yeah, Sherlock Holmes vibes). You've got a thousand clues scattered all over your office, but the clock is ticking. You need to solve the crime NOW. Suddenly, you've got this amazing assistant, who's way faster than you at sorting through clues, remembering details, and spotting patterns. They're like, "Hey, I noticed this footprint matches the tread on the missing person's shoe!" Boom. You solve the case way faster because your assistant did all the boring, brain-twisting stuff for you.

That's AI. It's like this super-smart detective helper that can look at piles of information (like photos, text, or data), recognize patterns, and give you answers. No coffee breaks, no whining. Just straight-up usefulness.

It's important to remember that AI isn't conscious or alive. It doesn't *feel* things or *want* things in the way a person or even a pet does. It's a computer program, but a very, very advanced one designed to perform tasks that usually require human intelligence, like understanding language, recognizing objects, or solving problems.

[Simple diagram idea: "How AI Works" - Shows three stages: 1) "Input" (question or data), 2) "Processing" (AI analyzing patterns), 3) "Output" (answer or result)]

How AI Learns New Tricks – Kind of Like a Dog

Now, here's where things get fun. AI isn't born super-smart. It has to learn. And it learns a lot like teaching a dog new tricks. Imagine you're teaching your dog, Sparky, to roll over. You give Sparky a treat every time they successfully roll over. Soon, Sparky figures out, "Oh cool, rolling over = treats. Got it." That's exactly how AI learns too, except instead of rolling over, it's learning how to recognize faces, translate languages, or predict what movie you might want to watch next.

Here's an example. Say you're trying to teach an AI program to recognize pictures of cats. You'd show it millions (like, MILLIONS) of cat pictures and say, "Yep, this one's a cat!" and "Nope, that's a dog wearing a weird hat." Over time, the AI gets better and better at figuring out which furry blob is a cat and which one isn't. Just like Sparky learns "roll over," AI learns "cat from not-cat."

This process is called machine learning. It means the AI gets smarter the more examples you give it. It finds patterns in vast amounts of data that humans might miss. It's like giving Sparky millions of different shaped objects and showing him which ones are round and which are square. Eventually, he'd get pretty good at spotting the round ones, even if you showed him a new round object he'd never seen before. That ability to learn from data and make predictions or decisions without being explicitly programmed for every single possibility is what makes machine learning so powerful.

[Simple diagram idea: "How AI Learns" - Shows three stages: 1) "Training Data" (many examples of cats and dogs with labels), 2) "Learning Process" (a simplified neural network with nodes and connections), 3) "Prediction" (new image being classified as "cat" or "dog")]

Think About It!

If AI learns from examples (like the dog learning "roll over"), what might happen if all the examples it learns from come from just one type of person or perspective? How might this affect what the AI learns?

Neural Networks – A Web of Ideas in a Brain-Like Web

Okay, this one might sound a little more complicated, but stick with me. You've got a brain (obviously), and your brain has something called neurons. Neurons are like little lights inside your brain that turn on and off to help you figure things out. For example, if you see a picture of, oh I don't know, a unicorn, different neurons light up to help you recognize that it's a horse with a horn (and that it's super cool).

AI programs use what's called a neural network, which is like a digital version of how your brain works. Instead of real neurons, it uses a web of math equations to connect ideas and make decisions. This web helps the AI figure out things like, "Hmm, this blob in the photo has a pointy ear, whiskers here, and it meows… it must be a cat!"

Think of it as a giant spiderweb connecting all kinds of information together. When information comes in (like the features of a cat's face), it travels through this web. Different paths through the web represent different patterns or ideas. The strength of the connections in the web changes as the AI learns (like Sparky getting better at rolling over). The stronger the connection between "pointy ears" and "cat," the more likely the AI is to correctly identify a cat. The more connections it makes, the smarter it gets. And just like a spiderweb, the bigger and stronger the network, the better it is at catching stuff—in this case, catching the right answer or making a useful prediction.

[Simple diagram idea: "Neural Network Layers" - Shows input layer (image of cat broken into pixels), hidden layers (nodes with connections of varying strengths), and output layer (classification: "99% Cat, 1% Dog")]

Modern AI, especially the kind that can generate text, images, or music, uses very, very large and complex neural networks, often called "deep" neural networks (because they have many layers of connections, making them "deep"). These are the kinds of networks behind tools you might have heard of, like the ones that power conversational AIs or AI art generators.

Try This!

Next time you use a device with a voice assistant (like Siri, Alexa, or Google Assistant), try asking it the same question in different ways. Notice how small changes in your wording can lead to different answers. This shows how AI tries to match patterns in language!

Why AI Isn't as Scary as It Sounds

Now you're probably thinking, "Wait, if AI is so smart, what can't it do?" I'm glad you asked! Here's the thing about AI: It's only as good as what it's trained to do. It might be awesome at recognizing cats, but ask it to tie your shoes, and it'll just sit there confused. AI doesn't *understand* things in the way a human does. It doesn't have personal experiences, emotions, or genuine creativity. It can combine existing information in new ways that *seem* creative, but it's not coming up with something truly novel based on feeling or inspiration.

AI doesn't have feelings, desires, or dreams (like, to become the first AI unicorn). It just follows the rules humans give it and the patterns it learned from its training data. It doesn't *decide* to do something; it calculates the most probable or optimal outcome based on its programming and data.

Humans are the ones who teach AI, and humans decide how to use it. That means you're in control of how this tool gets used. Treat AI like a friendly, laser-focused helper—not some spooky robot genius plotting an uprising. Just like a hammer can be used to build or break, AI's impact depends on the intentions and actions of the people using it and the people who created it. It's up to us to guide AI towards being a positive force.

Wrapping It Up

Alright, here's what we've learned in this first big step:

- AI stands for Artificial Intelligence and it basically means smart machines designed to do tasks that normally need human intelligence.

- AI is like a super-smart assistant that helps with tricky jobs by processing information fast.

- Machine learning is how AI learns, like teaching a dog tricks, by practicing with lots of examples.

- Neural networks are like brain webs inside AI programs that connect ideas using math to figure things out.

- AI is a tool, not a conscious being. It doesn't have feelings or independent desires.

That wasn't so scary, right? AI isn't magic or a monster. It's just a really handy, really smart tool. And now that you know the basics of what AI is and how it learns, you're ready to see how it's already showing up in your everyday life. Spoiler alert: You've probably already been using AI without even realizing it... but more on that in the next chapter!

Chapter 2: AI in Everyday Life – More Than Just Robots

Okay, you know AI is a smart assistant that learns. But where is it? Is it hiding in a secret lab somewhere? Nope! AI is already all around you, helping out in ways you might not even notice. It's like a helpful invisible friend making things a little easier.

Have you ever asked a smart speaker, like Alexa or Google Assistant, to play your favorite song or tell you the weather? That's AI! It understands your voice, figures out what you want, and makes it happen. This is called Natural Language Processing (NLP), a type of AI that lets computers understand human language.

Or maybe you watch shows or movies on services like Netflix or Disney+. How do they always seem to know just what you might like next? That's AI too! It looks at what you've watched before, compares it to what other people who like similar things have watched, and says, "Hey, based on what you like, you'll probably enjoy this show about talking animals!" This is recommendation AI, a very common type.

[Simple diagram idea: "AI Around Us" - A house cutaway showing different AI applications: smart speaker in living room, recommendation system on TV/tablet, spam filter on laptop, photo recognition on phone, navigation system in car]

Think About It!

How does the recommendation AI on your favorite video or music app guess what you might like? What clues do you give it when you watch, listen, like, or skip certain content?

AI is like a Librarian Who Knows Your Favorite Books (And Movies, And Songs...)

Imagine you go to a giant library with millions of books. Finding the perfect book would take ages! But imagine a super-smart librarian who remembers every book you've ever loved and knows exactly which other books are similar. You walk in, and they point you right to a pile of amazing stories you've never seen before. That's what recommendation AI does for movies, music, videos, and even products online. It learns your preferences and helps you find things you'll probably like, saving you time and effort.

Even something simple like your email uses AI. See that folder called "Spam"? AI helps filter out all the junk mail so you don't have to look at it. It learns what looks like real email and what looks like a scam based on patterns in words, sender addresses, and other details. This is a form of classification AI, sorting things into categories.

Try This!

Look at the apps on your phone or tablet. Make a list of which ones might be using AI and how (like photo apps organizing pictures, music apps suggesting

songs, or games with computer opponents). You
might be surprised how many use AI!

Here are a few more places AI pops up:

- **Self-Driving Cars (Getting Smarter):** Even cars
that aren't fully self-driving often use AI for things like
spotting obstacles, staying in lanes, or emergency
braking. They use computer vision (AI that "sees") to
understand the world around them.

- **Photo Apps (Recognizing Faces and Objects):**
Have you noticed how your phone's photo app can
group pictures of the same person together? That's
AI recognizing faces. It can also often identify
objects, like sorting photos of "dogs" or "mountains."

- **Online Shopping (Chatbots and Suggestions):**
When you ask a question on a website and a little
chat box pops up, sometimes you're talking to an AI
program called a chatbot. And when websites
suggest things you might also want to buy, that's
recommendation AI again.

- **Video Games (Making Characters Smarter):** AI
helps make the characters in video games seem
more realistic. It controls how enemies act, how
teammates help you, and how the game world
responds to what you do.

- **Translation Apps (Breaking Language Barriers):**
Apps like Google Translate use AI to understand

words and sentences in one language and turn them into another. While not perfect, they get better over time with more data.

So, next time you ask your smart speaker a question, get a movie recommendation, look through photos sorted by people, or use an online translator, remember: that's AI quietly helping you out. It's not future stuff anymore; it's right here, right now! It's woven into the technology we use every day, often working in the background to make things smoother or more convenient.

Chapter 3: Types of AI Tools You Might Encounter

Now that we know AI is around us, let's talk about the different *kinds* of AI tools you might see or even use yourself. It's like how there are different types of hammers – some for small nails, some for big projects. AI tools also come in different forms, designed for specific kinds of jobs.

[Simple diagram idea: "AI Tool Categories" - Shows four boxes: 1) Conversational AI (speech bubbles), 2) Creative AI (paintbrush and music note), 3) Research AI (magnifying glass with document), 4) Decision AI (checkboxes and arrows)]

Conversational AI (Like ChatGPT or Claude)

This is probably the type of AI you've heard the most about recently. Conversational AIs are programs you can talk to using text. They are trained on enormous amounts of text data from the internet – books, articles, websites, conversations – and they learn to predict what words should come next in a sentence to create human-like text. Think of them as incredibly advanced text prediction engines.

Analogy: Imagine the most well-read person in the world, who has also read every conversation ever written down. This person can discuss almost any topic and write in many different styles. That's kind of what a conversational AI is like, but without any actual understanding or feelings.

They are great for:

- Answering questions
- Writing different kinds of text (stories, poems, emails, code)
- Summarizing information
- Brainstorming ideas
- Explaining complex topics in simpler terms
- Translating languages (though often specialized tools are better)

Examples of tools in this category include ChatGPT (developed by OpenAI), Claude (developed by Anthropic), Gemini (developed by Google), and many others built into different apps and websites.

Research and Information AI (Like Perplexity AI)

While conversational AIs can answer questions, some tools are specifically designed to help you *find* and *understand* information from the real world, often citing their sources. These are built to act more like super-powered search engines or digital librarians.

Analogy: Imagine a librarian who can not only find books for you but can also read them instantly, pull out the key facts, and tell you exactly *where* they found that information in the book.

They are great for:

- Researching facts for school projects or hobbies
- Getting summaries of articles or topics with source links
- Exploring different viewpoints on a subject
- Learning about current events or historical topics

An example of this type of tool is Perplexity AI, which is designed to search the web and provide summarized answers with citations. Other conversational AIs are also adding or improving their ability to browse the web and provide sources.

AI Image Generators (Like Midjourney or DALL-E)

These tools are amazing! You type in a description of a picture you want to see (like "a cat wearing a spacesuit riding a pizza in outer space"), and the AI creates that image for you. They are trained on billions of images and their descriptions, learning how words relate to visual patterns.

Analogy: Imagine an artist who has seen every picture ever created and can mix and match elements from them to create something completely new based on your instructions.

They are great for:

- Creating unique artwork or illustrations
- Visualizing ideas for stories or projects
- Generating images for presentations or social media

- Just having fun seeing what crazy things the AI can draw!

Examples include Midjourney, DALL-E (from OpenAI), Stable Diffusion, and many others available online or integrated into apps.

Other Specialized AI Tools

There are many other types of AI tools designed for specific tasks:

- **AI Video Editors:** Help you quickly edit videos, add effects, or even generate short clips from text.

- **AI Music Generators:** Create original music based on the style, mood, or instruments you describe.

- **AI Language Learning Apps:** Use conversational AI or other techniques to help you practice speaking and understanding new languages.

- **AI Summarization Tools:** Specifically designed to take long documents, articles, or videos and give you the key points quickly.

Understanding that there are different types of AI tools, each good at certain tasks, is the first step to using them effectively. You wouldn't use a screwdriver to hammer a nail, and you wouldn't use an image generator to write an essay. Choosing the right tool for the job is key!

Try This!

If you have access (with permission if you're a kid!), try the same question with different AI tools. For example, ask both a conversational AI and a research AI: "What's special about tigers?" Compare how their answers differ.

Chapter 4: Practical AI for Kids (Ages 8-12)

Welcome back! Now that you know what AI is and some of the different types of tools out there, let's get practical. How can *you*, especially if you're around 8 to 12 years old, actually use AI to help you or have fun?

Remember, AI for kids is all about using these tools like helpful assistants or creative partners for learning and playing. The most common tools you might use are simple conversational AIs (like asking questions through a parent's account) or fun creative apps that have AI built-in.

Learning New Things with AI

Homework and learning can be more fun with AI! Imagine you're curious about something, maybe volcanoes, space, or how animals talk. Instead of just reading a boring old textbook (or searching through lots of websites that might be too complicated), you can ask a conversational AI tool a question.

Asking Questions for Homework Help:

You could ask a conversational AI tool, like one available through a parent's account:

- "What are the three main types of volcanoes?"

- "Tell me a cool fact about black holes."

- "Explain what photosynthesis is in simple words."

The AI can give you quick, easy-to-understand answers. It's like having a super-fast tutor who knows a little bit about everything. Just make sure you ask a grown-up for help and double-check the information in your books or with your teacher, because sometimes AI can make mistakes!

> ### *Try This!*
> Ask an AI to tell you a story about your favorite animal going on an adventure. Then try asking for the same story but in different styles – like "funny," "mysterious," or "like a fairy tale." See how the style changes!

Getting Creative with AI

Feeling stuck on a drawing or a story? AI can be a great way to get your imagination going!

Brainstorming Story Ideas:

You could ask a conversational AI tool:

- "Give me five ideas for a story about a magical dog."

- "What happens if a kid finds a portal to another dimension?"

- "Suggest some weird characters for a fantasy story."

The AI can give you unique ideas you might not have thought of! You can then take those ideas and make them your own. Remember, the AI gives you a starting point, *you* tell the real story!

Mini How-To Guide: Story Ideas with AI

Task: Creating Fun Story Ideas

Tool Type: Conversational AI (like ChatGPT or Claude)

Simple Steps:

1. **Think about your main idea:**
   - Pick something you're interested in! Like "underwater adventure" or "talking animals" or "space travel"
   - You might choose a main character too (a brave mouse, a silly alien, etc.)

2. **Ask the AI clearly:**
   - Type something like: "Can you give me 5 fun story ideas about a friendly dragon who can't breathe fire?"

- Be specific about what you want (how many ideas, what kind of character, etc.)

3. **Look at what the AI suggests:**
   - Read through the ideas
   - Pick one you like best, or mix parts from different ideas
   - You can even ask for more details about your favorite idea!

4. **Make it your own:**
   - Remember, these are just starting points – YOU are the real storyteller!
   - Add your own characters, twists, or settings to make the story special

Example:

What you might type:
"Give me 3 story ideas about a kid who discovers a magic backpack. The stories should be funny and have an adventure."

What the AI might answer:

1. A backpack that makes anything you put inside come out tiny! The kid accidentally shrinks their homework, pet hamster, and even their annoying little brother!

2. A backpack that can talk and gives terrible advice, leading the kid on a wild adventure through the town trying to find a lost puppy.

3. A backpack that can teleport the kid to anywhere they've drawn a picture of - but their drawings aren't very good, so everything looks weird and different from what they expected!

What you do next:

You might pick idea #2, but decide the backpack should give GOOD advice sometimes and BAD advice other times, making it more interesting. Then you start writing YOUR story with this fun idea!

Think About It!

How could AI help you learn something new that you're interested in? What questions would you ask it to help you understand a topic better?

Creating Fun Pictures:

Using an AI image generator (again, often with help from a parent), you can bring your wildest ideas to life. Want to see a dinosaur wearing roller skates eating ice cream? Just describe it!

You could ask an AI image generator tool:

- "Draw a fluffy pink cat with rainbow wings."

- "Create a picture of a castle floating in the clouds, drawn like a cartoon."

- "Show me a robot playing soccer with a dog."

These tools are fantastic for visualizing silly or fantastical ideas. It's like having a magic drawing machine that can create almost anything you can imagine!

Remember to Be Safe and Smart!

Using AI is exciting, but always remember these tips:

- Always use AI tools with a grown-up's permission and help, especially for things that connect to the internet.

- Don't share personal information with AI tools.

- Remember that AI tools can sometimes be wrong. Always check important facts with other sources, like books or trusted websites.

- Be kind and polite when using conversational AI, even though it's just a computer. It's good practice!

- Think of AI as a helper or a partner, not something that does all the work for you. Your brain is still the most amazing tool you have!

AI can be a super fun and helpful addition to your learning and creative adventures. Don't be afraid to explore (with a grown-up nearby) and see what cool things you can do!

Chapter 5: Practical AI for Teens (Ages 13-18)

Alright teens, school is getting more intense, projects are bigger, and there's more information out there than ever. AI tools can be incredibly powerful allies in helping you manage your workload, boost your creativity, and even explore future interests. Think of AI not as a way to cheat, but as a way to work smarter, just like using a calculator for math or a word processor for writing essays.

Supercharging Your Research and Learning

Instead of just using a basic search engine, specific AI tools can help you dig deeper and understand information better.

Conducting Research with Citations:

For research projects, especially when you need reliable sources, a tool like Perplexity AI can be fantastic. You ask it a question, and it gives you a summary *with links* to where it found the information. This is crucial for checking facts and citing sources properly for school papers.

You could ask a research AI like Perplexity:

- "What were the main causes of World War 1? Provide sources."

- "Summarize the plot of 'Romeo and Juliet' and list key characters with sources."

- "Find recent scientific findings about renewable energy and link to the articles."

This saves you time sifting through countless links. It's like having a personal research assistant who also hands you the books they used!

Mini How-To Guide: Research with AI

Task: Using AI for School Research Projects

Tool Type: Research AI (like Perplexity) or Conversational AI with citation capabilities

Simple Steps:

1. **Define your research question:**
   - Instead of broad topics ("World War II"), use specific questions ("What were the three main causes of World War II?")
   - Break complex topics into smaller, focused questions

2. **Ask the AI for information WITH sources:**
   - Type something like: "Explain the major effects of social media on teenage mental health. Please include reliable sources."
   - Be specific about wanting citations or sources in your request

3. **Evaluate the response:**
    - Look at both the information AND the sources provided

    - Check if the sources seem reliable (educational websites, known organizations, etc.)

    - Watch for any statements that sound questionable or don't have a source

4. **Verify the important facts:**
    - Click on source links to confirm they actually support what the AI claimed

    - For key information that will be central to your project, check at least 2-3 sources

    - If something seems surprising or too good to be true, definitely check it!

5. **Organize and use the information:**
    - Take notes in your own words based on what you've learned and verified

    - Create an outline with main points backed by confirmed facts

    - Always keep track of your sources for proper citation in your work

Example:

What you might type:
"I'm researching renewable energy for a science project.

What are the three most promising renewable energy technologies being developed right now, and what makes them special? Please include reliable sources."

How to use what you get back:

1. Read through the AI's explanation of each technology

2. Visit the sources it provides to verify the information

3. Look for any additional interesting points in those sources

4. Write your findings in your own words, citing both the original sources

---

Think About It!

How might you combine AI research tools with traditional research methods (like library books or interviews) to create a more complete and accurate project?

Summarizing Complex Information:

Got a long article or document for class that you need to understand quickly? Conversational AIs like Claude or ChatGPT can summarize it for you.

You can paste text (within privacy guidelines, of course!) and ask:

- "Summarize this article about climate change in three paragraphs."

- "What are the main arguments made in this passage about government?"

- "Break down this science concept into simple steps."

This helps you grasp the main points before you read the full text closely, or to quickly review study material.

Practicing a New Language:

Conversational AI can be an excellent practice partner for learning a new language. You can have a dialogue, practice grammar, or ask for vocabulary help.

You could ask a conversational AI:

- "Let's practice speaking Spanish. Ask me questions about my day."

- "Correct the grammar in this German sentence: [your sentence]."

- "Give me a list of 10 common French phrases for ordering food."

It's like having a language tutor available 24/7!

Try This!

Write a paragraph about any topic. Then ask an AI to help you improve it in specific ways – like "make it more formal" or "explain this more clearly" or "add

---

more vivid descriptions." Notice how it changes your writing while keeping your main ideas.

Boosting Your Creativity and Brainstorming

Whether it's for school projects, personal writing, or coming up with ideas for your YouTube channel, AI can break through creative blocks.

Generating Ideas for Projects:

Stuck on choosing a topic for an essay or a theme for a presentation? Ask an AI for ideas based on your interests.

You could ask a conversational AI like ChatGPT or Claude:

- "Give me 10 unique ideas for a presentation on marine biology."
- "Brainstorm themes for a short film script about friendship."
- "Suggest different angles to approach an essay about the impact of social media."

It gives you a list of starting points to get your own ideas flowing.

Drafting and Refining Writing:

AI can help you get started on writing or improve what you've already written. It can draft outlines, suggest different ways to phrase sentences, or help you expand on a topic.

You could ask a conversational AI:

- "Create an outline for an argumentative essay about whether school should start later."
- "Rewrite this paragraph to sound more formal: [your paragraph]."
- "Suggest ways to make the introduction to my story more exciting."

Remember, AI generated text is a starting point, not the finished product. Your voice and critical thinking are essential!

Creating Visuals for Projects or Fun:

Need an image for a presentation slide or a cool background for your phone? AI image generators can help.

You could use an AI image generator tool:

- "Create an abstract image representing complex data."
- "Generate a futuristic city skyline at sunset."
- "Make a cool logo idea for a coding club (include a circuit board and a book)."

Just be mindful of copyright and usage rights if you plan to share or publish images created by AI.

AI for Organization and Planning

Juggling school, hobbies, and social life is tough. AI can help you organize your time and tasks.

Creating Study Plans or Schedules:

Got a big test or multiple assignments due? An AI can help you break it down.

You could ask a conversational AI like Claude:

- "Create a study plan for my history test next week. I need to cover chapters 5, 6, and 7."

- "Help me create a schedule to finish my science project over the next four days, spending about an hour each day."

- "Break down the steps needed to organize a small school event."

It gives you a suggested structure, which you can then adjust to fit your real life.

Navigating AI Responsibly as a Teen

As you use more powerful AI tools, it's important to be responsible:

- **Fact-Check Everything:** AI can sometimes "hallucinate" (make things up). Never blindly trust information from AI; verify it using reliable sources.

Research AIs that cite sources are better for this, but still require you to check those sources.

- **Understand Plagiarism:** Using AI to write your entire essay without citing it or changing it is plagiarism. AI should be a tool to *assist* you in learning and writing, not a replacement for your own work and thinking. Your teachers can probably tell!

- **Be Mindful of Privacy:** Don't put highly personal information into public AI tools.

- **Develop Critical Thinking:** AI gives you information, but you need to think critically about it. Is it biased? Is it complete? What's missing? Your ability to *evaluate* information becomes even more important.

AI is a tool that can make learning and creating more efficient and fun. By using it smartly and responsibly, you can get a real advantage in tackling your busy life!

Think About It!

How might using AI tools change the way students learn in the future? What skills might become more important (like evaluating information) and what tasks might change (like memorizing facts)?

Chapter 6: Practical AI for Adults (Ages 19+)

For adults, AI is rapidly changing the workplace and offering new ways to manage personal life, pursue hobbies, and learn new skills. Whether you're working, studying, raising a family, or exploring new interests, AI tools can automate tasks, provide insights, and unleash creativity.

Boosting Productivity at Work

AI can take on many repetitive or time-consuming tasks, freeing you up for more complex and interesting work. Conversational AIs and specialized tools are particularly useful here.

Drafting Emails and Communications:

Staring at a blank email? AI can help you get started or polish your message.

You could ask a conversational AI like ChatGPT or Claude:

- "Draft a professional email to a client asking for updated project information."
- "Write a polite rejection email for a job applicant."
- "Help me phrase this tricky paragraph in a more diplomatic way: [your text]."

This saves time and can help ensure your communication is clear and professional.

Mini How-To Guide: Using AI for Professional Email Writing

Task: Crafting Effective Professional Emails

Tool Type: Conversational AI (like ChatGPT or Claude)

Simple Steps:

1. **Clarify your email purpose:**
   - Identify exactly what you need (request information, schedule meeting, provide update, etc.)

   - Note any specific tone needs (formal, friendly but professional, diplomatic)

   - Know who you're writing to (colleague, client, supervisor, etc.)

2. **Create a clear prompt:**
   - Specify the email type: "Draft a professional email to..."

   - Include key details: recipient type, purpose, any specific points to include

   - Mention tone preferences: "Use a friendly but professional tone" or "This needs to be formal" o Add context if needed: "This is following up on an unanswered request" or "This client is new"

3. **Review and personalize:**

o Check the AI-generated draft for appropriate tone and content

o Personalize with specifics only you would know (project details, personal connections)

o Remove any "AI-sounding" language that doesn't match your voice

o Ensure all details are accurate before sending

4. **Refine if needed:**

o If the first draft isn't quite right, give specific feedback

o Try: "Make this more concise" or "This sounds too formal, make it friendlier while staying professional"

Example:

What you might type:
"Draft a professional email to a client who has missed our last two invoice payment deadlines. I want to be firm but maintain a good relationship. Remind them of the payment terms (net-30) and ask when we can expect payment. This is a long-term client who's been reliable until recently."

After receiving the draft:

- Add specific details (invoice numbers, dates, amounts)

- Personalize the greeting with the client's name

- Adjust any language that doesn't sound like you

- Add your regular email signature

Try This!

Think of a task you find tedious or time-consuming. Research whether there's an AI tool that could help with it, or ask a conversational AI: "How could AI help me with [your task]?" You might discover useful tools you didn't know existed!

Summarizing Documents and Meetings:

Dealing with long reports, articles, or meeting transcripts? AI can quickly pull out the key points.

You can use conversational AI or specialized summarization tools:

- "Summarize the main findings of this 50-page report."

- "What were the key decisions made in the transcript of this meeting?"

- "Extract the action items from these meeting notes."

This is invaluable for quickly catching up or preparing for discussions.

Analyzing Data and Reports:

While complex data analysis often requires specialized software, conversational AI can help you understand reports or brainstorm ways to look at data.

You could ask a conversational AI:

- "Explain the key metrics in this sales report in simple terms."
- "Suggest different ways I could segment customer data to find patterns."
- "What are some potential reasons for a drop in website traffic based on these numbers?"

It can help you ask better questions about your data or understand analyses provided by others.

AI for Personal Life and Learning

Beyond work, AI can simplify daily tasks, aid personal growth, and enhance hobbies.

Planning and Organizing Personal Projects:

Planning a party, a home renovation, or learning a new skill? AI can help structure your efforts.

You could ask a conversational AI like Claude or ChatGPT:

- "Help me plan a schedule for renovating my kitchen over four weekends."

- "Create a checklist for planning a child's birthday party for 10 kids."

- "Outline a roadmap for learning basic guitar chords and simple songs over two months."

It breaks down big tasks into smaller, manageable steps.

Learning and Skill Development:

Whether it's a new language, a coding skill, or understanding a complex historical event, AI can be a powerful learning aid.

You could use conversational AI or language learning apps:

- "Explain the concept of blockchain technology in a way a beginner can understand."

- "Generate practice problems for learning Python programming loops."

- "Roleplay a conversation in Italian where I am ordering coffee at a cafe."

AI provides personalized explanations and practice opportunities.

Enhancing Hobbies and Creativity:

From writing to art to cooking, AI can be a creative partner.

You could use conversational AI or image generators:

- "Give me ideas for a mystery novel setting."
- "Suggest variations for a chocolate chip cookie recipe using ingredients I have: [list ingredients]."
- "Create an image of a peaceful forest scene with glowing mushrooms."
- "Write a short poem about autumn leaves."

AI can spark new ideas or help you visualize concepts.

Think About It!

In your job or daily responsibilities, what tasks require uniquely human abilities (like empathy, creativity, or ethical judgment)? What tasks are more routine and might be augmented or changed by AI tools?

Researching and Exploring Topics:

For personal curiosity or important decisions, research AIs are valuable.

You could use a research AI like Perplexity AI:

- "What are the pros and cons of installing solar panels on a house? Provide sources."

- "Summarize the history of jazz music and recommend five influential artists."

- "Find information about different types of indoor plants that are easy to care for and safe for pets, with sources."

This provides quick, source-backed information to help you learn or make informed choices.

Using AI Responsibly as an Adult

The principles of responsible AI use apply even more strongly when dealing with professional or personal decisions:

- **Verify Information Rigorously:** Especially for health, financial, legal, or critical work tasks, *never* rely solely on AI-generated information. Always cross-reference with trusted, authoritative sources.

- **Protect Sensitive Data:** Be extremely cautious about entering confidential work information or highly personal details into general-purpose AI tools. Understand the privacy policy of any tool you use.

- **Understand AI's Limitations:** AI lacks true understanding, empathy, and nuanced judgment. Don't use it for tasks requiring human sensitivity, complex ethical decisions, or situations where factual accuracy is paramount without human oversight.

- **Avoid Bias:** Be aware that AI models can reflect biases present in the data they were trained on. Critically evaluate AI outputs, especially when they involve people or sensitive topics.

- **Use AI to Enhance, Not Replace:** AI is most powerful when used to augment human capabilities, not simply replace them. Focus on how AI can help you do your job *better* or free you up for higher-level tasks.

AI offers tremendous potential for adults to improve efficiency, unlock creativity, and make informed decisions in many areas of life. By approaching it as a powerful assistant and using it thoughtfully, you can harness its benefits while navigating its challenges.

Chapter 7: Addressing the Big Questions About AI (Revisited)

Alright, let's talk about some of the worries you might have heard again, now that you know more about what AI is and how it's used. If AI is so smart and helpful, could it also be... dangerous? Will AI take over the world? Will robots take everyone's jobs?

These are big questions, and it's good to think about them. But remember what we learned in Chapter 1? AI is a tool. It doesn't have feelings or evil plans. It does what humans tell it to do, based on how it was trained.

[Simple diagram idea: "AI and Jobs" - Shows three categories: 1) "Jobs changing with AI assistance" (doctor using AI for diagnosis, writer using AI for research), 2) "New AI-related jobs" (prompt engineer, AI ethics advisor), 3) "Jobs requiring uniquely human skills" (therapist, creative director)]

AI is Like a Hammer—It's a Tool, Not a Decision-Maker (Still True!)

Think about a hammer. A hammer is a really useful tool! You can use it to build amazing things, like a treehouse or a bird feeder. But you could also use a hammer to break something, or accidentally hit your thumb (ouch!). Is the hammer evil? No! It's just a tool. How it's used depends on the person holding it.

AI is exactly like that. It's a powerful tool. Most people building and using AI want to use it for good things – helping doctors find illnesses, making cars safer, finding solutions to climate change, creating tools for learning and creativity. But like any tool, it *could* be used in ways that aren't helpful, or even harmful, if a person chooses to do that or if the AI is built poorly. The important thing isn't that the AI itself is bad, but how humans decide to build and use it, and how we build safeguards and ethical guidelines around it.

The scary stories about AI taking over often imagine AI developing consciousness or independent desires, which is still firmly in the realm of science fiction. The AI we have today is designed for specific tasks and relies on vast amounts of data and computing power to perform those tasks. It doesn't wake up one morning and decide it wants to rule the world.

Try This!

Have a conversation with friends or family about AI. Ask them what they're excited about and what concerns them. Compare their thoughts with what you've learned in this book. Do they have misconceptions you can help clear up?

What About Jobs?

This is a more realistic concern than robot uprisings. Historically, new tools and technologies have always changed the kinds of jobs people do. When cars were invented, fewer people worked with horses, but new jobs were created building and fixing cars, building roads, and selling gas! The internet changed jobs in retail and information, but created countless new jobs in web development, digital marketing, and online services.

AI will probably change some jobs too. Tasks that involve lots of repetition, sorting through huge amounts of data, or generating basic drafts of text or images might be partly done by AI. But it will also likely create new jobs that we can't even imagine yet, jobs where humans work *with* AI. Think of prompt engineers (people skilled at telling AI exactly what to do), AI trainers, AI ethicists, and roles that combine human creativity, strategy, and empathy with AI's processing power.

Humans have creativity, critical thinking, empathy, and complex problem-solving skills that AI doesn't. These human skills will be even more important in the future. Instead of thinking about AI "taking over," it's more accurate to think about humans and AI *working together*, each doing what they are best at. Humans set the goals, ask the questions, guide the process, and make the final decisions. AI helps process information, find patterns, generate possibilities, and do tasks faster.

Change can be unsettling, but societies have adapted to major technological shifts before. The key is to focus on learning new skills, understanding how to work *with* AI, and ensuring that the benefits of AI are shared broadly.

Think About It!

How do you think AI might change society in the next 10 years? What changes would you be excited to see, and what would you want humans to be careful about?

It's okay to be thoughtful and cautious about new technology. We need to make sure AI is built and used fairly, safely, and ethically. Discussions about AI bias, privacy, and security are important. But the scary stories in movies are just that – stories! The real AI is a tool, and humans are in control of how it's built, guided, and used.

Chapter 8: The Exciting Future of AI (And Why It's Bright)

So, if AI isn't going to take over the world, what *is* it going to do? The future of AI is actually full of really exciting possibilities that could make the world a better place.

Think back to the idea of AI as a super-smart assistant. As AI gets even smarter and more capable, it can help us tackle some of the biggest challenges humanity faces.

AI Helping Us Stay Healthy

Imagine doctors being able to spot illnesses like cancer much earlier by using AI to analyze medical scans super fast and with incredible accuracy, sometimes noticing tiny details a human eye might miss. Or imagine AI helping scientists discover new medicines and treatments for diseases by quickly analyzing massive amounts of biological data. This is already starting to happen! AI can process huge amounts of medical information, drug compounds, and patient data much quicker than a human can, speeding up research and diagnosis.

AI can also help with personalized medicine, understanding why certain treatments work better for some people than others based on their genetic information and health history.

Try This!

Imagine you're living 20 years in the future. Write a short "day in the life" story about how you might use AI tools throughout your day. Be creative but realistic based on what you've learned!

AI Helping Our Planet

AI can also help us protect our planet. Scientists are using AI to understand climate change better, predict weather patterns more accurately (which helps with preparing for natural disasters), and find new ways to create clean energy. AI can help manage energy grids efficiently, optimizing where power comes from (solar, wind, etc.) based on demand and weather. It can also help monitor forests for signs of trouble like illegal logging or fires, track endangered animal populations, and design more sustainable materials.

AI is a powerful tool for understanding complex environmental systems and helping us make better decisions to protect Earth.

AI Making Life Easier and More Accessible

What about making life easier for everyone? AI is helping develop amazing tools for people with disabilities. Imagine AI-powered apps that can describe what's happening around them for visually impaired people, narrating scenes or reading text aloud. Or tools that help people with communication difficulties speak or write more easily. AI translation is getting better all the time, potentially breaking down language barriers so people from different countries can communicate more freely.

AI could also help develop more personalized education, tailoring learning materials and pace to each individual student's needs and style. In our homes, smart devices using AI will continue to make daily tasks more convenient, from managing your grocery list to optimizing your home's energy use.

Think About It!

What problem in the world do you think AI could help solve? What kinds of data would the AI need to learn from, and how would humans and AI need to work together?

Humans and AI Working Together

The most exciting future isn't about humans vs. AI. It's about humans *using* AI as a partner to solve some of the world's biggest challenges and unlock new possibilities. AI can do the number-crunching, pattern-finding, and repetitive tasks, while humans bring the creativity, critical thinking, empathy, ethical judgment, and big-picture vision. Together, we can do amazing things that neither humans nor AI could do alone.

Think of AI as a new superpower we're just learning to use. Like any superpower, it needs to be used responsibly and guided by human values, but the potential for good is enormous! By understanding AI and participating in discussions about its future, you can help shape this exciting new chapter.

www.ingramcontent.com/pod-product-compliance
Lightning Source LLC
LaVergne TN
LVHW012333060326
832902LV00011B/1873